Standards Based Education:

Steps to Success in Implementing a Standards - Based School or Program

Contents

Introduction v

Chapter 1
Standards: What Do They Really Mean? 1

Chapter 2
Maintaining Effective ECE Programs 7

Chapter 3
Where Do You Start? 15

Chapter 4
Aligning Standards with the Development Domains 21

Chapter 5
Teaching Strategies 31

Chapter 6
Aligning Curriculum with Standards:
An Interdisciplinary/Integrated Thematic Unit
for the Second Grade 41

References & Resources 59

Aa Bb Cc Dd

Introduction

When I was approached to research and write a publication, I first thought, "I'm the last person to address this subject." However, as an educator with over 30 years of experience in the education field, I decided that I had some perspective that might be useful to other educators as they struggle with maintaining the basic philosophy of early childhood education while implementing a standards-based program. This book addresses standards-based school reform in effective early childhood programs and classrooms. It asks and answers these questions:

- How are the two similar?
- Can we change as early childhood educators and include a standards-based program while maintaining the basic premises of Early Childhood Education (ECE)?
- How does this change appear to the school, teacher and children?
- What are the benefits to children in this process?

Coming from a philosophy of developmental early childhood education at Arkansas State University with the mentoring of Dr. Mildred Vance, I was taught to develop a passion for doing what's good for children and to consider how children learn and grow according to Piaget and a host of other developmental experts including Froebel, James Hymes, and Maria Montessori. I was taught that teachers should develop curriculum and environments that meet children's individual needs and provide school experiences where children can be successful as they learn and grow. *Children learning through play and sensory experiences was our motto.*

Having been around when the Arkansas State Legislature voted to implement and fund public school kindergarten in the early 1970's and being a first year kindergarten teacher in one of the first state funded classrooms, my charge was set forth. I was there to keep kindergarten pure and different from the rest of the elementary school.

Throughout these thirty years, staying pure and different has meant many things for early childhood teachers and programs. Holding on to the basic premises about child growth and development has been invaluable and being a life-long learner a necessity. But, most importantly, being a person who can take risks and look for the positive in change has served me well. In Joan Lunden's book, *Healthy Living*, she visits the power of positive thinking in our lives. "Focusing on the positive things in your life will help you cope with the challenges." *Change is a challenge!*

ECE teachers must become involved and participate in new education movements:

- to establish safeguards in effective early childhood teaching methods.
- to ask essential questions.
- to develop age appropriate curriculum.
- to utilize appropriate assessments for young children.
- to maintain standards as benchmarks to improve schools and enhance children's success.

All the new research in brain growth, curriculum, strategies and methods is fascinating. But with it comes a responsibility to use it in our everyday lives with children. It might mean adding something new, or it could mean giving up something we like. But if it's good for children, do we have the choice to say NO? We have the responsibility as early childhood education professionals to be on the cutting edge. There is no place for victims in our profession, only problem solvers.

Many opportunities have presented themselves over the years in my early childhood career. Many people are responsible for these opportunities coming my way. Some of my most memorable professional growth experiences were made in programs that at the beginning I was not sure were good for children. The children and families touched by these programs demonstrated that they were successful and opportunities to contribute to those programs became my challenge.

I'm not saying it will always be easy. Remember in the movie Mary Poppins tried to get Jane and Michael to clean up the nursery after a hard day of play. The children were fussing about the work and Mary Poppins broke into a

What Can You Do?
- Bring to the table your expertise about child growth and development.
- Prove what is best for children by trying new ideas.
- Be involved in research.
- Make recommendations on how to improve ideas and strategies.
- Monitor the children in your care to make sure they have the best education.

Recipe for "Medicine Sugar"

One cup of **looking for the good** in what we are about to do.

Two cups of **surrounding ourselves with people with positive attitudes.**

Three cups of **learning all we can** about new ideas and asking questions.

Four cups of a **support system** of family, friends, and colleagues

One cup of **celebration for success.**

Introduction

song...'Just a spoonful of sugar helps the medicine go down..." Mary Poppins brought to the situation a positive attitude with a little magic and music, the right motivation for Jane and Michael to change their attitude and have fun. *Change* is a medicine that can help us do better and that sugar can motivate us, support us, be the positive we need to make the change, and the celebration for success.

Our charge is here. We'll explore the positives of standards-based programs and how standards can work with the premises of effective early childhood education. **It's time to give it a go!** If this is a change for you, take a lesson from the F.I.S.H. philosophy, *Fresh Ideas Start Here* (2001).

- CHOOSE YOUR ATTITUDE.
- PLAY. Involve yourself and others around you in plenty of play this shouldn't be hard considering most of them are young children.
- BE PRESENT. Get involved with the work you have to do and be heard.
- MAKE THEIR DAY!

Do more for your children. More may mean new, different, standards....success. We're all in this together!

Chapter 1

Standards:
What Do They Really Mean?

> **STANDARDS** are defined as "a comparison of human performance to a standard."

My first thought was "here we go again..." Standards-based education (SBE) isn't a new concept for many of us who have stayed around for several decades. As with many educational programs, SBE has cycled through a few times. Each time it changes with research, experiences, successes and failures. It only makes sense that there would be more information than had been seen previously as it came to the front of the educational scene in the 1990's. As with all programs, philosophies, strategies, and curricula, it was certain there would be some components that would fit with basic early childhood knowledge and beliefs. Our work as early childhood educators became clear to find the matches between effective early childhood programs and standards-based education and start there.

Characteristics of Standards-Based Education

○ **Standards are built on the premise that all children can learn but all children are different.**

Believing this premise is not enough. Teachers and administrators must support the premise on a daily basis in every classroom. Children have many different needs, from glasses to insulin to more time for specific tasks. Teachers who differentiate instruction to children are very aware of the differences in children. Standards set high expectations for all children. A goal is set and all children work toward that goal at his/her own pace.

Ee Ff Gg

When the goal is mastered, success is earned. If mastery is not achieved, more time and work are made available until mastery is earned. *Failure is not accepted: work ethic is built.*

- **Standards are the same for all children.**

Traditionally, we have denoted success in school with letter grades or a test that uses a bell curve. Grades in school are determined with percentages from assignments given by teachers. What one teacher grades as "A" might not be graded by other teachers as "A." Emotion plays a part in the grading system. The individual teacher considers both the attitude of the student and the difficulty of the assignments and these perceptions can vary from teacher to teacher. In standards-based classrooms, mastery of skills is the expectation for all children.

In Standards-Based Schools:

- Standards are set and assessments are developed.
- Instruction leads straight to the assessment.
- Performance, observation, portfolios are used as part of the assessment and instruction.
- Performance is the name of the game.
- Differentiated instruction is necessary to enable every child to be successful. The goal may be the same, but children are at different places in the learning process.
- Time, instructional technique and strategy may differ with students.
- Flexible groupings may be necessary for efficiency. Similar ability groups for teaching needed skills allows the teacher to differentiate teaching within classroom time constraints when individual instruction cannot be managed.
- All children participate with teaching including higher-order thinking skills (HOTS).

Reeves, Douglas. (2002) *The leader's guide to standards: A blueprint for educational equity and excellence.* San Francisco, CA: Jossey-Bass Publishing.

Reeves, Douglas, (1998). *Standards, Assessments, and Accountability,* An Address through the Arkansas Department of Education, Center for Performance Assessment.

Standards: What Do They Really Mean?

❍ **In standards-based schools and classrooms "It's not how you start but how you finish."**

What's the most important question?

- *Has he mastered the standard?* or
- *How quickly has he mastered the standard?*

I love to use my son as an example of this. It seems that we seldom start the new six week period with A's and B's. The first grades seem to be at the other end. So, WE (he and I) hustle to bring up the low grades during the remainder of the period to have a decent grade on the report card. He always learns the material and does the assignments, but to the beat of his own drum, a slower beat than that of his peers. In the end he knows the material like everyone else but his grades may be lower. Grades on a report card are simply an average of all the grades turned in within a determined time period and are not a true reflection of what the child has learned or mastered.

❍ **Scoring guides are developed for the standard and all children are measured against the same criteria.**

Standards are not measured on a bell curve. Children are not in competition with each other. Everyone has an equal chance to excel. It's not "Can I do it more quickly and better than someone else?", but "Can I learn the standard? Can I succeed?" Because children are not in competition with each other, teamwork and cooperation are encouraged and successful reinforcement is given by class members.

Isn't it amazing how children follow the teacher's lead and example in attitudes and actions toward each other? Encouragement should be the name of the game in our homes and classrooms. Children love to celebrate the smallest successes for each other. They help each other with the right modeling from the adults around them. Celebrations can happen with a pat on the back, verbally, good notes or certificates, positive phone calls to parents by child and teacher together, special treats or activities, etc.

❍ **Standards are fixed.**

The bell curve approach on standardized tests does not allow all children to be at the top, and the top changes with each administration of the test. Children are in competition with each other. Only a few will reach the highest points of curve, but many will be average. The highest students may actually know more some testing periods than other testing periods. Isn't it possible for all children to master the standards if they are appropriate? Shouldn't all children have the chance to be successful?

Ee Ff Gg

> **Can you match these early childhood principles with the criteria for Standards-Based Education?**
>
> - All children can learn.
> - All children are not the same.
> - Teachers set high expectations for children.
> - All children should have the opportunity to learn at their pace.
> - All children should have the opportunity to be successful.
> - Children should learn teamwork and cooperation rather than compete against each other for success.
> - Teachers should work as a team to develop the school or district standards.
> - Professional development for teachers should be a priority.
> - Accurate information about the success of children for parents, students, the community and teachers should be used for improving teaching and learning.
> - Children should have the opportunity to demonstrate knowledge frequently throughout the year and all teachers and administrators should grade consistently.

- **Standards are more accurate.**

With standards it is more important to measure a few important concepts several times during the course of the year than assessing many concepts once. In some situations, placements for children are determined by a single test score or **High Stakes Testing**. Standards-based programs allow children to be assessed throughout the year many times. The assessments are tied to the standard. Performance assessments used with standards allow children to demonstrate knowledge and understanding in a variety of ways: verbally, writing, models, projects, presentations, etc. Multiple-choice tests are not used because of random guessing.

- **Assessments should always improve teaching and learning.**

There are no hidden agendas. The scoring guide is given with the assessment so children know what is expected. Samples of proficient and advanced work are considered and displayed for all to see. Standards are visible in classrooms. The results of these assessments are used to make decisions on how to help children. This information is then communicated to parents, children, and the community to accurately reflect what children really know.

Standards: What Do They Really Mean?

- **Standards are developed by grade level teachers in each school or district using the state frameworks as a guide.**

Standards reflect what the important concepts for that grade will be in each content area. In order to accomplish this, teachers and administrators align the curriculum continuously, looking for what is actually being taught versus what should be taught. Teachers of similar and different age and grade levels have conversations and collaborate to have consistent and relevant goals for children. Priority is given to staff development for all staff in developing scoring guides and using them consistently among teachers and administrators.

How Do We Know This Really Works? Where's the Proof?

Research was conducted on schools that have "beat the odds." (Marzano, 2002) These schools are high poverty schools with students who do not have strong home support systems. In spite of these strong indicators for academic failure, all schools demonstrate high student achievement.

The research demonstrated that all of these schools included the standards-based characteristics mentioned above. Shouldn't all of us look closely at what effective schools are doing? How do we match and how are we different? What are you doing that I'm not doing? How can I get where you are?

In summary, we can say that standards are academic benchmarks or grade level curriculum measured by scoring guides, decided upon by school and district teachers using the state and national frameworks. Standards are fair, consistent, clear, accurate, effective and constant.

Notes

Chapter 2

Maintaining Effective ECE Programs

> "POTENTIAL NEGATIVE EFFECTS OF NATIONAL STANDARDS INCLUDE THE THREAT TO BOTH INTEGRATED CURRICULUM AND EMERGENT CURRICULUM, THE RISK OF EXPECTATIONS BECOMING STANDARDIZED WITHOUT REGARD FOR INDIVIDUAL AND CULTURAL DIFFERENCES, AND THE DANGER OF ESTABLISHING INAPPROPRIATE PERFORMANCE STANDARDS.....VOICES OF EARLY CHILDHOOD EDUCATORS, ESPECIALLY THOSE WITH PARTICULAR DISCIPLINARY EXPERTISE AND INVOLVEMENT IN THE SUBJECT-MATTER ORGANIZATIONS, MUST BE HEARD IN THE DEBATE."
>
> Bredekamp & Rosegrant (1995)

In order for standards to be a successful support for children, teachers, and schools, work must be done to ensure that early childhood principles are maintained. Two organizations have developed resources that are critical guides for the implementation of standards in the early childhood setting and appropriate outcomes in each content area. The National Association for the Education of Young Children (NAEYC) and the National Association of Early Childhood Specialists in State Department of Education (NAECS/SDE) have published resources that lay out the safeguards and role of teachers of young children in implementing standards-based classrooms. *Reaching Potentials: Appropriate Curriculum and Assessment for Young Children* Vol.1 (1992) and *Reaching Potentials: Transforming Early Childhood Curriculum and Assessment* Vol.2 (1995), edited by Bredekamp and Rosegrant, interpret, apply, and elaborate with specific content goals from *Guidelines for Appropriate Curriculum and Assessment For Young Children Ages Three to Eight*, published in 1992 by NAEYC and NAECS/SDE.

We must remember that national standards drive state standards that guide district and school standards. Involvement and problem solving begin at the national level and continue down to the school and district. Victims complain and wait, but offer nothing to the movement. Our role is to ensure that effective strategies like integrated curriculum, play, and cultural differences become part of the standards curriculum. Standing firm on the appropriate ways to assess children as outlined by NAEYC and other early childhood experts is a safeguard for our children. Becoming sensitive and bringing these issues to the forefront will keep our early childhood teaching effective.

> "BECAUSE STATE STANDARDS ARE HIGHER STAKES THAN NATIONAL STANDARDS, THEY REQUIRE EVEN MORE CAREFUL EVALUATION AND SCRUTINY AGAINST GUIDELINES SET BY THE EARLY CHILDHOOD PROFESSION."
>
> Bredekamp & Rosegrant (1995)

Higher stakes at the state level include "merit pay for teachers, funding and control of school districts, and individual children's futures." As teachers, planning a curriculum with appropriate and meaningful standards, assessments, and activities for your children is your ethical responsibility. Participating on committees at the school level to develop standards and curriculum alignment, giving feedback to local representatives of organizations such as the Southern Early Childhood Association and its state and local chapters, keeping abreast of and sharing the current research through education journals and publications are ways to be involved in what happens with the children you care for and teach. Your voice does count!

Teaching the Wrong Things at the Wrong Time

David Elkind, in his book *Miseducation* (1987), warns teachers to be careful of teaching "wrong things at the wrong time." Particular attention needs to be paid to what the child needs to learn, not what the

Essential Questions to Ask About Young Children's Curriculum

- Is this content worth knowing?
- Is it meaningful and relevant for these children's lives?
- Can it be more relevant by relating it to children's lives?
- Can children gain direct experience with it?
- Is the content accurate and credible according to the recognized standards of the relevant disciplines?
- Are the expectations realistic and attainable at this time, or could the children more easily and efficiently acquire the knowledge or skills later on?

adult wants to teach. This behavior can put the child at risk. Infants and young children need large amounts of time for "exploring and understanding their immediate world." Elkind explains that John Dewey went further when he said, "Learning is the representation of experience." Elkind elaborates that talk and reflection about the experience are part of the learning cycle.

Using the Effective Components of Teaching

Levine in *A Mind At A Time* (2002) spends much time discussing the importance of teacher summarizing and student paraphrasing after presenting information for developing memory in children. Teachers of young children provide a time and place for exploration and learning, but must be involved in guiding the learning environment, using all the effective components of teaching.

Setting Realistic Goals

In his book *Developmental Education in an Era of High Standards*, (Modern Learning Press, 1998), Jim Grant defines standards as "an approach to teaching that matches the curriculum and methods of instruction to a child's current stage of development and individual needs." Developing appropriate standards must involve a consideration of child growth and development and utilization of strategies to individualize instruction. Effective standards allow realistic goals, and time to reach these goals for all children.

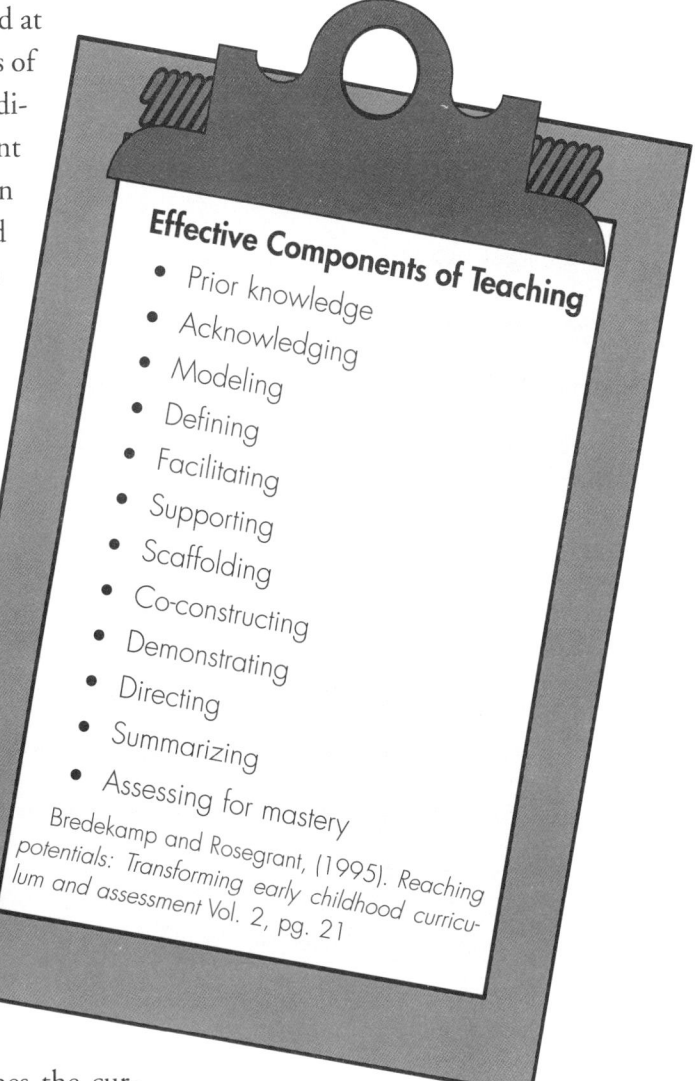

Effective Components of Teaching
- Prior knowledge
- Acknowledging
- Modeling
- Defining
- Facilitating
- Supporting
- Scaffolding
- Co-constructing
- Demonstrating
- Directing
- Summarizing
- Assessing for mastery

Bredekamp and Rosegrant, (1995). *Reaching potentials: Transforming early childhood curriculum and assessment* Vol. 2, pg. 21

Success at Each Level of Schooling

Creating the Total Effective School (Lazotte, 1992) states that "students master knowledge and skills that are essential prerequisites for success at the next level of schooling." This always reminds me of the analogy my mom used when she sold World Book Encyclopedias ages ago. In her sales pitch, she said that educating children was like building a cathedral. You start with the basement, then begin the floor of the church, building all the way up to the belfry and steeple. Without a good foundation the steeple and church will topple over. Provide children with the educational experiences they need to meet their needs today, and they will be ready for tomorrow.

Incorporating Effective ECE Strategies in Classrooms

Many of the strategies traditionally found in early childhood classrooms such as circle time, learning centers, active learning, exploration with plenty of time for play, integrated curriculum, small group and individualized teaching, Higher Order Thinking Skills (HOTS), *Bloom's Taxonomy*, parent involvement, portfolios, observation, and performance assessments can be used effectively in standards-based classrooms. ECE teachers have always had the challenge of matching child growth and development to teaching methods and readiness skills. Teachers of young children should not resort to paper/pencil test book practice but should continue using appropriate materials and strategies. To prepare children for the next step, educators must meet the children's current needs and capabilities with appropriate materials and methods. Grant (1998) explains that the pressure of standardized testing spreads downward on lower grade teachers so they focus on future learning rather on the student's current needs.

I am always proud to tell the story of the first grade master teacher who remained true to early childhood principles and reading research when required to make a compromise. The first year that she finished her training for "model" status in a balanced literacy program, she was required to use a standardized pre/post test as one of the many forms of assessment with her children. To put it mildly, we were not happy with this rule and protested vehemently to the powers that be, all to no avail. We were committed to the literacy program and proceeded as directed, but cautiously.

A control group from the same school population was also tested on the standardized test with both groups scoring in the 50th percentile on the pre-test. The master teacher stayed true to her methods and never swayed from her conviction that if she taught the children with correct methods and materials, they would perform well on the standardized test as well as on the other assessments. When the results were returned, her children scored at the 84th percentile on the post-test. The control class scored again at the 50th percentile on the post-test after many sessions of "preparing for the test." For the last three years, her children have been just as successful as the first year. Although required to utilize an assessment tool that she didn't consider appropriate, she managed to incorporate those early childhood strategies that she knew were best for children, stayed true to her philosophy and was successful in meeting accountability standards.

This story reminds me of my own years as a kindergarten teacher. The first grade teachers really liked for kindergarten children to use a readiness workbook and assessment with the basal reading program. Well, I just couldn't do it, so we opted for a Big Book version of the workbook. I must say we had wonderful fun with it in a rather short period of time, and I taught literacy skills, alphabet and letter-sound connections in a developmental, meaningful way with lots of poems, songs, manipulatives, and language experience stories the children wrote. When we'd take the "test", those kindergartners would whiz right through with no trouble at all! Worked every time.

Setting Standards Based on the Actual Capabilities of Today's Children

In *Early Education and The Elementary School Principal Standards of Quality Programs for Young Children*, 2nd Edition (1998) the National Association of Elementary School Principals (NAESP), recommends that standards that are "derived from texts and tests, rather than actual capabilities of today's children" should be prevented. With the current research on brain growth and learning in young children, new strategies and techniques in all areas of development enable children to master some skills earlier than previously thought. Caution should be observed to ensure the learning standard is relevant, meaningful and applicable to children.

Recently the developer of a national ECE curriculum and assessment program asked our district to participate in the norming process for a new ECE math assessment for three and four year old children. We accepted the opportunity to be involved, curious as to what the new assessment included. Two of the local Head Start classrooms participated. The teachers were asked to critique the assessment as they administered it individually to the children and include comments. The most relevant comment was that the teachers expressed surprise at all the math skills and concepts the children had mastered. They had no idea their children could perform as well as they did and were thrilled with the information the assessment had given. They developed a new awareness of what their curriculum had accomplished to support their children's success and activities that could further challenge the children were included in the curriculum.

Improving the Performance of Students and Schools

Standards should be compatible and result in school success, rather than ideology and statistics. "They are effective and meaningful guideposts that improve performance of students and schools." Physical, intellectual, social, and emotional aspects of development should be addressed in the ECE curriculum. Young children should have a wide range of language and literacy experiences to enhance cognitive development and build a foundation for reading instruction.

The National Association of Elementary School Principles (NAESP) recognizes that children between the ages of 3 and 8:

- Are in a state of rapid mental growth and development.
- Need many direct sensory encounters.
- Can benefit from teacher directed instruction.
- Seek out stimuli to nourish mental abilities.
- Should develop a strong sense of self-esteem.
- Flourish in direct learning experiences most of their instructional day.
- Should be in an environment that allows them to develop an excitement and curiosity for learning.

Instead of teachers and administrators asking, " Is the child ready for school?", they should be asking, **"Is the school ready for the child?"**

At the 2002 Annual Conference of the School of the 21st Century at Yale University, Rosa Smith, in a keynote address, proclaimed the absolute necessity of appropriate early childhood education for all our children. Smith's answer is to do away with high schools and use that money for pre-school education, based on her belief that "if we did early education through eighth grade correctly, high schools, as we know them today, would be obsolete, redundant, and boring..." Rosa continues that, "Meaningful and quality academic results for all children will occur only when we create an education system that puts into practice what we already know about child development and the importance of early education." Her message was loud and clear that as professionals we have the responsibility to love children enough to not let them fail.

Several times over the years a "wild child" kindergartner has shown up on the first day of school with literally no social, intellectual, emotional and physical skills: skills needed to succeed in kindergarten. Many times, the teacher wanted to tell the parents to keep their child at home another year to mature so the child will be ready for kindergarten the following year. I could never understand how the child would be more mature if he had already spent five years in that home environment. Why shouldn't the child spend the time at school with a trained, skilled teacher and the support system and resources of the entire school, along with parenting help for the adults at home to become more supportive of the child? We can make a strong case for early identification of at-risk children, quality pre-school experiences for the child at school or home and parent education to promote school success.

Support Systems for Teachers

The school must address the important question of what support systems and professional development opportunities are in place for the teacher. Accessibility to a full array of services and resources for student and teacher are necessary for success.

Providing staff development and planning time for teachers to learn and support each other as it relates to standards, curriculum alignment, best practice, technology, appropriate assessments, student achievement, and parent involvement is imperative. Opportunities for teachers to receive training and information must be organized and planned carefully. Many teachers spend their own time attending seminars and workshops; however, there are some professional development opportunities that the school needs to attend together and some specific sessions that individual teachers need. Differentiating staff development is necessary to have that great school. Teachers should have a process for recommending topics for staff development. Resources should be available for staff to attend conferences that directly impact their teaching and to have the materials and supplies necessary to implement after they return from the training. Discussions should take place between staff members about the implementation.

Sharing with other members of the staff should also occur. A certain level of accountability to implement should be expected. Accredited centers and schools have minimum requirements for staff development classes or hours. Many schools are now giving monetary incentives to teachers for attending hours above the minimum requirements. All of these strategies ensure the success of the teachers in implementing the standards.

Standards-based schools continually plan, instruct and assess a standard until every child has mastered the standard. Teachers and administrators never stop or give up on a child: they just continue to give the child every opportunity to succeed. No Child Left Behind leaves no space for giving up on a child. That is why it is so important to keep up with best practices, brain research and researched strategies. If you keep doing what you have always done, you will have the same results you have always had.

Notes

Chapter 3

Where Do You Start?

You've probably already started. Most states have already written standards for early childhood education. You, your center or your school need to access them. Many are posted on web sites through the State Department of Education or Department of Human Services. In fact, many states have several publications, not only with the standards but also with activities and explanations for home or classroom. Find them!

When you have the set of state standards in hand, you and other teachers at your center or your school are ready to begin the real work of writing standards specifically for your children. To be effective in teaching and working with children, the standards must be in place to serve as a guide for your classroom activities and lesson plans. Mastered, they are the pot of gold at the end of the rainbow.

Writing Standards for Your Program or School

> *A COMMITTEE CONSISTING OF TEACHERS, COMMUNITY PARTNERS, PARENTS, ADMINISTRATORS, AND AN EARLY CHILDHOOD SPECIALIST OR CONSULTANT MAKES A REPRESENTATIVE GROUP FOR WRITING AND APPROVING STANDARDS.*

The state or national guidelines are just that, guidelines. Standards should be written for your individual school or center and have buy-in from all stakeholders. This isn't the easiest part of a teacher's work or the most fun you will have in the teaching/learning process. Most teachers love curriculum planning for children. They enjoy the delivery of curriculum with activities that successfully engage children through work and play. But, to be successful, teachers have to know what the end result should be for classroom activities, and children must have time to learn and practice these skills. So, dig in and get the job done.

> *THERE SHOULD BE CONTINUITY BETWEEN AGE LEVELS OR GRADES AND CURRICULUM ALIGNMENT THROUGHOUT A PROGRAM OR SCHOOL. IN OTHER WORDS, THE SKILLS AND CURRICULUM SHOULD FLOW FROM ONE AGE LEVEL OR GRADE TO THE NEXT.*

There should be a natural overlap, but repeating the exact skill over and over should not be necessary if the skill is appropriately placed. Discussions between teachers of different grades, classes etc., are mandatory to find gaps and overlaps. If everyone ignores a certain skill or standard because they don't like or know how to teach it, that creates a gap. If the same standard is taught repetitively for several years, overlap occurs.

One school in the process of writing standards for their school district had third and fourth grade teachers disagreeing over who should teach multiplication and division. Third grade teachers wanted to teach multiplication through the tens and no division. Fourth grade teachers wanted to teach multiplication and division on the six through ten facts and have third grade do the same for zero through five facts. Without the discussion and cooperation of teachers in both grades, gaps in teaching multiplication and division would have occurred. Who is responsible for these decisions and continuity in curriculum? Teachers and stakeholders, and they were at the table doing their job!

Teachers have always used topics of interest through **integrated units**, such as dinosaurs, to help children learn skills. Motivation in the teaching/learning process is key. Several years ago, most classrooms from pre-K to sixth grade had a major dinosaur unit planned during the year. Every year children learned many of the same facts about dinosaurs. Teachers spent many days, weeks, etc., discussing facts about dinosaurs. Yes, children were building vocabulary, making comparisons about the different kinds of dinosaurs, measuring dinosaurs, talking in complete sentences using adjectives to describe dinosaurs, and older children were researching and writing paragraphs. Many standards were being practiced by using the study of dinosaurs as a motivator. Most of theses activities were appropriate for children. Teachers took a hands-on, sensory approach with the units. Children were indeed motivated. But several problems came to the forefront.

- Teachers could not describe the end result or goal of the dinosaur unit (essential questions) and how their unit in kindergarten differed from the one the second grade teacher was using.
- Assessment of the essential questions was not consistent and defined. How were these essential questions assessed?
- The same activities were being done year after year.
- Parents could not understand why the children were doing the same activities and could not see the difference in content.

Where Do You Start?

- Children were not being introduced to other important topics because there was not enough time in the school day and year.
- Administrators began thinking that integrated units were a waste of time, and too much "fluff" was taking valuable time away from other standards and skills.

Integrated units are one of the most effective teaching and learning strategies that teachers can use with children. The challenge is for early childhood teachers to face these issues and learn from the mistakes being made. When standards are in place, the essential questions of each unit are driven by the standards to be taught. Indeed, the problem of the same units coming up year after year is no longer a factor in the learning process. Teachers must leave behind some favorite units and activities to make room for the standards that need to be taught. If the standards are appropriately aligned, the decisions are black and white for the teacher. Emotions can't be used to decide what to teach.

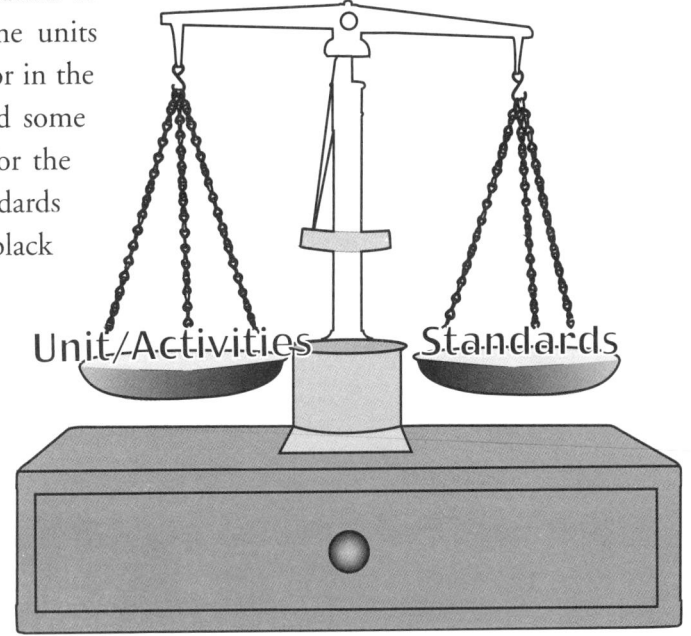

The same problems arise when the same skill is taught year after year with no difference in the end result. For example, one common skill you will notice in language is the study of nouns. Nouns are taught each year from elementary through junior high. The overlap is noticeable to parents and children. What are the differences each year? Do they warrant an intensive amount of time year after year? As teachers discuss the standards at each age or grade they are refined and some may be eliminated at different grades, leaving more time for the essential standards at that grade to be learned and practiced.

In the big picture, there are many motivating subjects in science and social studies that our children should have an opportunity to learn about. To spend teacher time each year on the same subject is not expanding children's vocabulary and providing enough varied experiences. Children are capable of learning about many subjects.

> *A STRONG EARLY CHILDHOOD EDUCATION BASE AND PHILOSOPHY OF PROMOTING GROWTH IN ALL DOMAINS IS MORE EFFECTIVE IN SUPPORTING LEARNING AND COGNITIVE DEVELOPMENT FOR ALL AGES AND GRADES. PROGRAMS THAT FOCUS ONLY ON THE COGNITIVE DOMAIN OR READING AND WRITING SKILLS ARE MISSING THE POINT OF QUALITY EARLY CHILDHOOD EXPERIENCES AND SUCCESS FOR CHILDREN.*

Building the framework for standards is like building that cathedral we talked about earlier. A strong, broad basement supports each level as the child learns and grows. Maslow's (1970) hierarchy of needs demonstrates the basic needs of love and security along with food, clothing and shelter before cognitive learning is attained. The old stories of the child coming to school hungry needing to be fed or from a household fight between mom and dad, needing to talk to his teacher or the counselor before he can attend to his spelling lesson still are pertinent examples of how basic needs take precedence over higher needs. All domains or areas of development (social-emotional, physical, cognitive, language, and creative/aesthetic) must be addressed in the standards for ECE to be appropriate.

As an administrator for kindergarten classrooms, year after year I saw children come to school who knew the alphabet and maybe even some words. But, many could not use manipulatives, were embarrassed to sing in a group, did not know rhymes and fingerplays, cried if they had to draw a picture or person without a color sheet to color in the lines, had trouble galloping, walking a balance beam or other skills that should be part of a child's development. Over and over research has shown the positive effects of experiences in music, the arts, and physical development on the cognitive development of young children. Do you have the right as teacher, administrator, or parent to ignore this information? **NO**. The best and highest quality programs for children include all domains or areas of development in their standards.

> STANDARDS MUST BE ASSESSED BY TEACHERS AND TAUGHT TO CHILDREN WITH APPROPRIATE STRATEGIES, TECHNIQUES, AND ACTIVITIES.

This is what "beginning with the end in mind" means. We know the expectations. They are written in the standards. We plan our assessments to determine if the child has mastered the standard. Assessments for young children include portfolio development, teacher observation, parent observation, performance assessments, and testing that is done one- on- one with the same manipulatives that children use in their environment. School- age children often are tested with reading inventories and running records in reading to know the correct reading levels for instruction to be effective.

Once the assessment is selected, the curriculum or roadmap is developed to give every child opportunities to learn. Each skill or standard should provide the opportunities for children to work at the concrete, associative, and memory levels of learning. Children younger than five will always work more at the concrete and associative levels; however, opportunities should be given for children to try the memory level. Kindergarten children always read pictures before words and should always have many opportunities at concrete and picture association before moving to the paper/pencil memory level. Second graders and older children should have opportunities to learn at the concrete level with manipulatives before the paper/pencil tasks. Standards cannot stay on paper and be effective. *They must be used to plan curriculum: they must come alive.*

Where Do You Start?

"Best Practice" or teaching strategies developed with a researched base are the determining factor in selecting strategies, techniques, and activities. Planning, creating the learning environment, selecting strategies for delivering instruction, guided practice, center activities, cooperative group activities, assessment, and all other components should be selected carefully. Resources are abundant for teachers to use in planning, assessing, and teaching. In today's information age, lesson plans are just a click away; however, just because it's on the Internet or in a book does not mean it is good for children or will help children master a standard. Be careful in using activities, techniques, or strategies that have no research, recommendation from early childhood experts, NAEYC, SECA, or other recognized professional groups. Use your team of teachers or teacher support group to brainstorm and bounce ideas off each other.

> *THE COMMITTEE CONTINUES TO STUDY WHAT IS ACTUALLY BEING TAUGHT TO CHILDREN AS COMPARED TO WHAT THE STANDARDS SAY, MAKES RECOMMENDATIONS FOR CHANGES AND RECOMMENDATIONS FOR STAFF DEVELOPMENT.*

"Weeding the garden" becomes a function of the committee. That means getting rid of skills, activities, integrated units that serve no real meaning in teaching standards to children at that age, level, or grade. Placing the right standards at the right age for children is a continuous process. Select and plan carefully for success.

Notes

Chapter 4

Nn Oo Pp

Aligning Standards with the Developmental Domains

Children should have opportunities in all developmental domains at home and in the classroom. Following is a sampling of the types of experiences in each domain that should be included in your standards. We've taken the information from the Arkansas Early Childhood Education Frameworks, but your state will have the same type of state standards that you can use to customize your local standards to your school, children and state.

Social-Emotional Domain

Children should have opportunities to:

- feel safe and depend on their parents and teachers.
- demonstrate a curiosity for learning and a confidence to try new things.
- work and play alone and with other children.
- express their ideas and feelings.
- learn appropriate social behaviors (character traits such as honesty and cooperativeness, manners, how to treat friends).
- learn to take care of their own needs independently (learning to dress themselves, wash hands and face, brush their teeth properly, use the bathroom, use a Kleenex).
- make choices (choose toys or centers they would like to play with, friends to do things with).
- accept responsibility for their behavior (admit if they make a mistake and what they can do to correct the mistake or make others feel better about their mistake).

- become an important part of the family or class by contributing to the group (feeling a part of the family and class, being responsible for small chores, and using their talents).
- see appropriate modeling from the adults at home and at school.

Excerpted from the Arkansas Early Childhood Education Framework, 1996

There are wonderful character education and behavior management programs available for teachers and parents. Standards-based schools continually look to best practice and research-based programs for effective programs to meet the needs of their children. If your school or program has a Parent Center, it may have many resources available to parents and offer parent study groups to interested parents on relevant topics. If your school or program has a Professional Development Center or Coordinator, you'll find many resources for teachers there.

Some Suggestions for Successful Character Education and Behavior Management Programs

Character First Program, a program that utilizes parents as volunteers in school to help teach a curriculum on character traits weekly in classrooms.

Love And Logic Program, by Jim Fay, an excellent resource and training curriculum offered to both parents and teachers on managing behavior with natural consequences for children.

Stop And Think, a behavior management program that includes a social skills curriculum for children by Howard Knoff, Florida State University.

Physical Domain:

Children should have:

- healthy snacks and meals prepared each day.
- plenty of exercise and movement, transitions (poems, fingerplays, songs when moving from one activity to another activity), indoor and outdoor play, and rest scheduled throughout their day.
- a clean, safe environment at home and at school.
- activities that give practice in handling blocks, cubes, puzzles, and Legos for stacking and building; beads, and spools for stringing; crayons, and pencils for drawing; scissors for cutting; buttoning, zipping, tying for dressing themselves and their dolls; spoons, forks and knives for eating and preparing their own snacks.
- activities that develop skills in identifying their body parts, moving their bodies in different

Aligning Standards with the Developmental Domains

directions, walking, marching, jumping, galloping, skipping, running, throwing, catching, balancing, kicking, pedaling.
- activities that promote cooperation and team support combined with motor coordination with little or no focus on competition.

Excerpted from the Arkansas Early Childhood Framework, 1996

Physical education classes for young children should focus on warm-ups, games, and motor skills that later can be adapted into team sports. More effort and encouragement should be placed on developing a risk-free environment where all children enjoy participating in recreation than on competition between children. Children should be receiving P.E. several times during the week from elementary physical education certified teachers and daily follow-ups from their classroom teachers. Recess alone does not provide the best program for children, but certainly is a piece of the daily schedule that provides time for children to make choices and practice motor, social-emotional, cognitive, language, and creative domains. A standards-based sequential program with instruction and guided practice from trained teachers gives children the opportunity to develop life-long recreational skills and enjoyment.

Brain research is continually showing how children need access to water, exercise and snacks to maintain focus throughout the school day. Teachers should take seriously the availability of water, healthy snacks and exercise for children. Physical and occupational therapists insist that children should have transitional exercises like chair push-ups, spider crawling, or sit-ups throughout the day. I am always reminded of the miserable feeling I get as I try to sit at a conference for a long period of time. Friends around me usually get notes, drawings, ideas passed between us, or they can see me half-drugged trying to keep my eyes open until we can move. If adults can't sit for an hour without getting sleepy or antsy, how can we expect children to do the same thing? We all need those brain pick-me-ups: water, healthy foods and exercise.

Cognitive/Intellectual Domain

Children should have the opportunity to:
- Enjoy listening to, reading and talking about books, stories and many types of literature.
- Hear, understand, and use many words.

Nn Oo Pp

- Develop their problem-solving skills and creativity.
- Build skills in recognizing differences and similarities in objects.
- See relationships between and among ideas and words.
- Build memory and recall for events, people, and ideas.
- Manipulate letters, shapes, and words.
- Understand that print conveys a message and uses writing for a purpose.
- Build shape, color, letter, and letter-sound recognition and relationships.
- Demonstrate an understanding of number, numeral, addition and subtraction, measurement, geometry, data, algebra, multiplication and division using manipulatives and, later, abstract thinking.
- Show pride in family, heritage and background.
- Learn about other cultures and compare to their own.
- Use safe behavior and be responsible in caring for the environment.
- Understand the role of people in our world.

Excerpted from the Arkansas Early Childhood Education Framework (1996), NKARP 21st Century Conf (2002) and Teaching Our Youngest: a Guide for Preschool Teachers and Child-Care and Family Providers (2002)

"Cognitive development is the basis for all human learning ..." (Dorothy Strickland, White House Summit on Early Cognitive Development, 2001) Throughout each day children should be playing language, rhyming word, number, and spatial concept games with each other and with adults. They must have time for talking to and with children and adults. Children should be using language to talk, to learn about letters, sounds, words and to write. A balance of time should be spent in **teacher-directed large group, individual and small group instruction,** and **independent work times.** All of these techniques are effective best practices when used at the appropriate times. Teachers should be skilled in **questioning techniques** and able to use them throughout the day. When questioning is appropriate and effective children are able to practice higher levels of thinking. Giving children the answer to problems is not

always the best way to help them learn. Being able to ask the right question to give children opportunities to think at higher levels allows them to problem solve and grow cognitively.

One day in our kindergarten class, a group of children was in the block center trying to build a highway with the unit blocks for the new wooden cars that had arrived the day before as part of the transportation unit we were studying. Quite a discussion began when they didn't have any more long blocks to finish the project. They couldn't agree to all work on the same project and share. Imagine that?!

It would have been easy for me to say as a teacher that two of the shorter blocks are the same as one long block or for the boys to work on one highway instead of two. But, instead, I asked for suggestions on how they thought we could finish the project. They kept saying they needed more blocks. So I asked," Can we make a long block from anything else we have?" One child suggested paper. One child suggested small blocks, and they began to put blocks together and measure. Quickly they came up with their own solution (two blocks making one) and the project was completed successfully.

Language Domain

Children should be able to:

- Demonstrate effective oral communication with sentence formation, grammar, expressing feelings and information.
- Carry on a two-way conversation with others.
- Participate in songs, poems, fingerplays, and rhymes.
- Use language to problem solve.
- Listen and follow directions in sequence.

Excerpted from the Arkansas Early Childhood Education Framework, 1996

As a parent I remember my two-year-old daughter and her love for stories and books. She would bring me the same books over and over until she quoted them from memory. Later, this memorization process was carried over to videos. One day we were at the grocery store and she was riding in the basket. As we went through the aisles of the store she started reciting from Tikki Tikki Tembo. Other people in the store thought she was speaking some foreign language as she recited "Tikki Tikki Tembo. No Sa Rembo, Chari Bari Ruchi, Pik Perri Pembo, He's at the bottom of the well." Later for several weeks she would dramatize the whole story with her dad, explaining which character he should be and teaching him the right words to say. (It made a pretty good play. By the way, Dad was always at the bottom of the well.)

The daily schedule must include many opportunities for children to talk, discuss, share, summarize, and paraphrase. In reading, we have always said that it's necessary for children to read books to become good readers. Programs like *Accelerated Reader* (AR) have research to support this concept and teachers are using *Accelerated Reader* and *Drop Everything And Read* (DEAR) with wonderful results.

Whether you are playing the piano, basketball hoops, gymnastics, or cooking, "Practice Makes Perfect." Children must practice language to perfect their skills. Teachers have so much to share and offer children with good language as they teach throughout the day. Children need opportunities to say it back and

Making It Happen!

First grade Writing Center; share writing with a friend

Kindergarten lunch program

Kindergarten nature walk writing & collage

Parent Volunteers in Cabot Schools aid teachers in the production of literacy materials

Photographs courtesy of Ward Central Elementary, Ward, Arkansas.

Parents & Pre-school children are special guests two mornings a week for play activities & lunch/play groups

First grade Spelling Center with magnetic letter match

Rhyming picture game in the Poetry Center; cooperative play at the semi-concrete level

Rhyming words chart at the Abstract level/writing rhyming words

Rhyming at the concrete level

First grade small group writing instruction

practice that vocabulary, sentence structure, grammar, style and content. They also need opportunities to reconstruct the message in their own words, say what they understand, give others information, and communicate their feelings.

Not only do they need to say it, they need to draw and write it! Large group instruction should always include summarizing from the teacher, paraphrasing from students, sharing and discussions. These strategies not only increase language development: according to Levine (2002), they increase memory skills in children. Children should have opportunities to work in pairs and in cooperative groups. Recess and lunch should offer opportunities to socialize with other children and adults. Teachers facilitate the environment to have the time in the daily schedule for providing opportunities for children to develop language.

Creative Domain

Children should be able to:

- Use imagination, participate in dramatic play with dress-up and props.
- Enjoy singing and experiment with a variety of musical instruments.
- Explore and use a variety of art media, creating drawings and paintings with detail.
- Recognize and respond to beauty in their environment.

Excerpted from the Arkansas Early Childhood Education Framework, 1996

Aligning Standards with the Developmental Domains

One of the favorite activities in my kindergarten classroom was the "Happy Trash Box," a decorated box of all the scraps of paper and leftover art project supplies accumulated throughout the year. I raided the workroom and begged other teachers for supplies. I always had a stack of poster board templates from projects. My mom sent leftover fabrics, trims, buttons and laces from her sewing projects. The children loved contact paper scraps and stickers. Stamps were a big hit too. Each morning during center time children would look through the box and begin putting together collages, pictures, or reproducing the art projects they had made on previous days. All domains were practiced in the art center with the Happy Trash Box!

Notes

Chapter 5

Teaching Strategies

Setting the environment for young children and facilitating learning is the role of the teacher. All children must be allowed time, experiences and support at school and home to be successful. Teachers in standards-based schools employ many teaching strategies to assist students.

Differentiated Instruction

Standards-based schools differentiate to help all children master standards. It is not accomplished in one prescription or lesson plan for all children, but by **differentiating the instruction** to meet the need for each child.

As children are observed and assessed, an **academic plan** is used to make sure the child's needs are being met. Most children are ready to work on the standards that are appropriate for their age or grade level. However, some children need additional practice, additional time, specific types of instruction or modifications. Other children are ready to move at a faster rate, participate at higher levels of curriculum or with enrichment activities. Large group instruction falls short with these extremes in children.

The teacher's role is to establish an environment where every child is motivated and learning. Many effective teachers use **small group instruction** for "like-skill needs" rather than trying to teach all children individually. Teachers of young children work with a group of four to six children needing the same practice or instructional level.

Qq Rr Ss

Cooperative Learning groups are used with elementary age children with grouping that includes all levels and types of learners so that peer interaction gives all levels of children an opportunity to use their strengths. Children can learn from each other. Some children respond well to working with another student in pairs to do research on subjects and projects.

Writer's Workshop, Step Up To Writing and other similar writing programs allow each child to complete each stage of the writing process at individual rates of time. Teachers work on a schedule throughout a specified time frame to provide individual time and instruction to each child. All children succeed at their level of writing proficiency. Teachers find similar needs in children and have small or large group instruction times as needed.

Some Strategies to Consider in Differentiating Instruction

- **Stations or Independent Learning Centers**—Provide enrichment and reinforcement in exploring topics in depth.
- **Acceleration and Curriculum Compacting**—Encourages teachers to assess students at the beginning of a unit of study or standard. Students who have mastered the information or skill move on to other skills or standards, spend time studying a topic normally not available for study or complete an independent study.
- **Complex Instruction**—The teacher asks higher order thinking, open-ended questions, initiates peer discussions and follow-up questions.
- **Entry Points**—Howard Gardner used several techniques to explore a topic: presenting a story, using numbers, studying vocabulary, hands-on activities, and sensory characteristics.
- **Independent Studies**—Independent research over a period of time with supervision, teaching and guidance from the teacher.
- **Problem-Based Learning**—Students actively solve problems related to the topic.
- **Choice Board**—Assignments are on a board or pocket chart set up by the teacher for students to have choices controlled by the teacher.
- **Flexible Grouping**—All students have the opportunity to work with students that have both similar and different abilities and interests.

Sources: *The Differentiated Classroom: Respond to the Needs of All Learners* by Carol Ann Tomlinson and Dr. T. Roger Taylor in *Differentiating the Curriculum Using An Integrated, Interdisciplinary Thematic Approach*.

Teaching Strategies

Guided reading in balanced literacy programs allows for children to read at their "level" with other students at the same level in a small group of four to six children. In guided reading groups, children receive direct reading instruction from a trained teacher in reading, writing, and spelling. They learn strategies for reading and writing, practice daily and are assessed weekly. Groups are flexible and children move at their own pace through the levels, changing groups as needed.

Some children are identified by IDEA or have 504 plans written to address specific learning problems. These children may have written modifications that classroom teachers are required to follow. Other children are not identified or do not qualify under these programs; however, specific strategies, learning styles instruction, or modifications to the teaching/learning process may be needed in order for these children to be successful. Parent communication is very important in these situations. Parents should be involved in any accommodations or modifications occurring in the classroom. Teachers should document behaviors and academic and behavioral accommodations for the parent.

Learning Centers

Daily scheduled **learning center time** and independent active learning time provide children with opportunities to practice skills they have been taught or introduced to, but have not yet mastered. Centers are an effective way to manage children in practice with sensory, manipulative learning, and discovery play. Children work/play at their skill level.

LEARNING CENTERS

Teacher Selected
- teacher selected activities
- children have opportunities to practice in all centers
- usually includes cognitive areas: may include all areas of development

Both (overlap)
- daily practice of taught skills or frameworks
- manipulatives, hands-on activities
- management system in place
- social & language development opportunities

Free Play
- children choose activities they prefer to work and play – self-esteem developed
- teacher facilitates environment to include all cognitive areas, modalities and areas of development
- discovery learning

Qq Rr Ss

There are two types of learning centers. Both allow children to work together and give all children the opportunity to be successful each day!

- *Teacher's Choice* uses center time to have children work/play on specific activities or materials. Children may make choices of when or what order they wish to complete the center activities.

- *Free Play* is a scheduled time in early childhood classrooms that allows children to choose the centers and activities they would like to work/play in. Choice promotes a positive self-image as children usually choose activities with which they are successful and work with children with whom they enjoy socializing.

In both types of centers there are management systems in place to make the classroom organized and safe for all children. Management systems vary according to a teacher's likes and dislikes. Some teachers have children rotate or follow a schedule on a management board. Other teachers have children move a marker or clothespin to the center as they move in order to control the number of children at the center. In both systems, children should be responsible for cleaning up and taking care of materials.

The materials in the center are selected carefully to be versatile for many levels and are changed throughout the year to motivate children to be successful. Centers are also a management system for children to work and play while the teacher is providing direct instruction to small groups of children. Designated, labeled areas for children to move to for different domains or subjects are set up around the classroom.

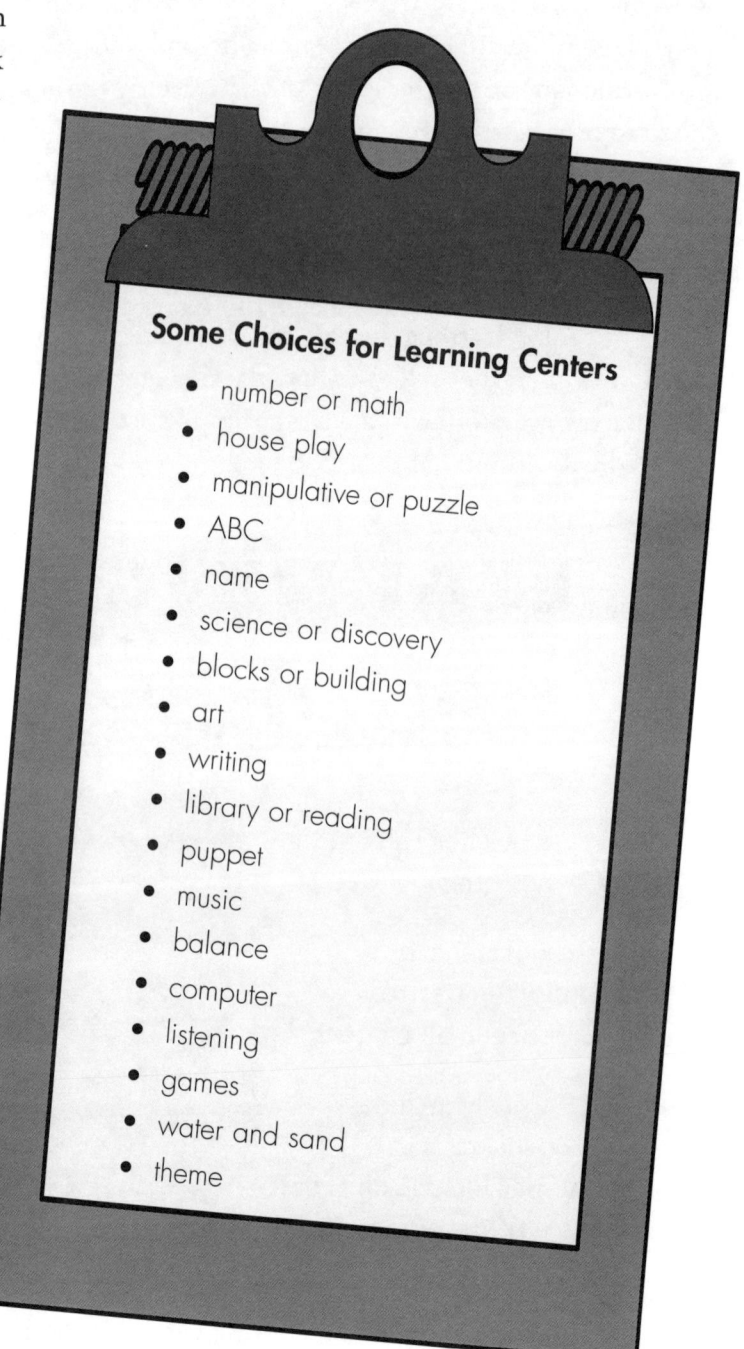

Some Choices for Learning Centers
- number or math
- house play
- manipulative or puzzle
- ABC
- name
- science or discovery
- blocks or building
- art
- writing
- library or reading
- puppet
- music
- balance
- computer
- listening
- games
- water and sand
- theme

Teaching Strategies

There are many resources to assist you in setting up learning centers in ECE classrooms. They provide options for set-up such as room arrangement and lists of appropriate materials and supplies for each center. *Creative Curriculum* and *Picture This: A Framework for Quality Care and Education For Children Three to Five* are examples of some resources.

In situations where space is a problem, teachers may elect to have tubs or baskets with hands-on activities for children to take back to their table or seat and work; however, remember that tables are more conducive for active learning projects and sharing.

Children use learning centers to practice activities and to be involved in active learning, both with peers and independently. Learning centers should be filled with manipulative and active learning projects for children, and they should change throughout the year to give children opportunities for varied learning experiences.

In literacy programs, learning centers are sometimes referred to as Literacy Corners. Specific tasks are set-up in each area for children to practice literacy skills. Some include ABC, Word Building with Magnetic Letters, book baskets of familiar reading, listening, charts and poems. If children have had appropriate centers in ECE, they transition to Literacy Corners easily.

Direct Instruction

The role of the teacher is to facilitate the classroom environment and learning. Direct instruction is one of the effective strategies used by teachers. Research dictates specific components of an effective lesson. Direct Instruction includes many steps. Beginning with the child's background knowledge, the lesson should include stating the objective, definitions, explanation, modeling, demonstrating, summarizing, checking for understanding, practice both guided and independent, assessing, re-teaching and assessing. *Pathwise*, (Arkansas, 1995) a newer training program available to teachers and administrators, also addresses effective components of the teaching process.

> DIRECT INSTRUCTION CAN BE USED IN LARGE GROUPS, SMALL GROUPS, AND INDIVIDUALLY. LARGE GROUP INSTRUCTION IS THE MOST EFFICIENT USE OF THE TEACHER'S TIME, IF THE INSTRUCTION IS PERTINENT TO ALL CHILDREN. THE MORE STUDENT INVOLVEMENT THAT IS USED IN DIRECT INSTRUCTION, THE MORE APPROPRIATE IT IS FOR YOUNG CHILDREN. TEACHING IS NOT TELLING. TEACHING IS USING MANY STRATEGIES TO INCLUDE THE LEARNING STYLES OF ALL THE CHILDREN IN THE GROUP AND ALLOWING CHILDREN TO PRACTICE THE SKILL WITH SUPERVISION FROM THE TEACHER.

Visual, tactile and auditory modalities should be used in direct instruction. Many teachers use overhead projectors, power point presentations, posters, charts, pictures, Big Books, film clips, songs, recordings, etc. to involve all types of learners. Young children spend time in teacher directed instruction at circle time activities and small group instruction times. Older children have more direct instruction

Qq Rr Ss

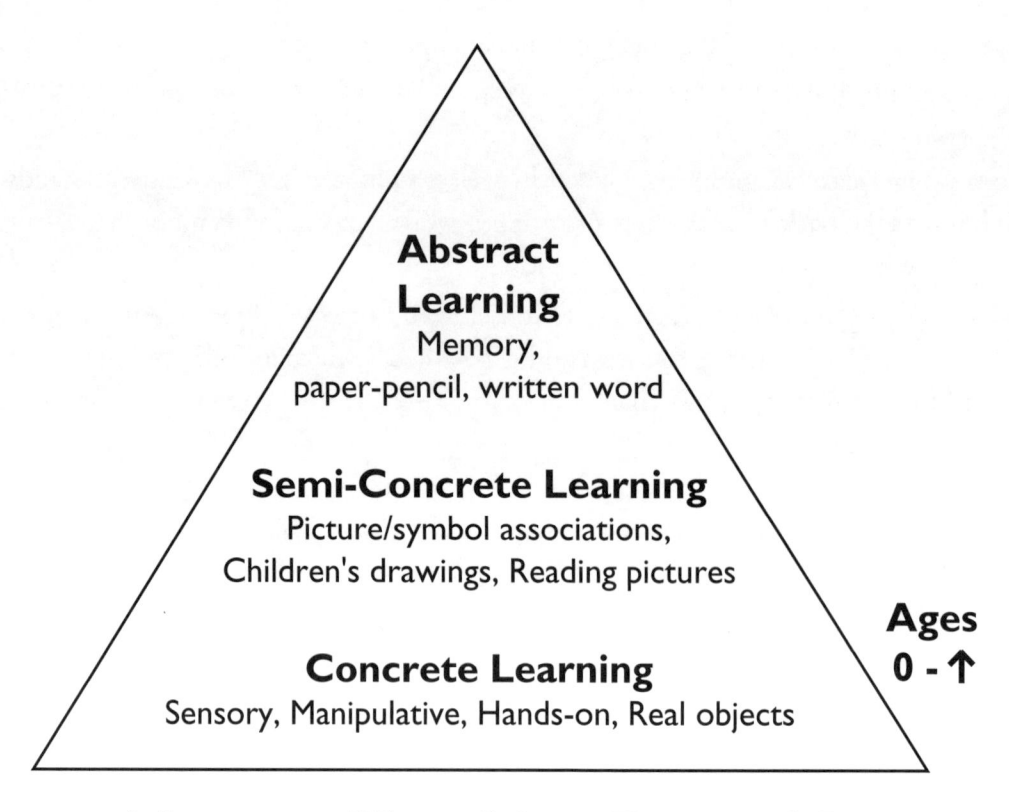

```
          Abstract
          Learning
          Memory,
     paper-pencil, written word

       Semi-Concrete Learning
         Picture/symbol associations,
      Children's drawings, Reading pictures

         Concrete Learning                      Ages
   Sensory, Manipulative, Hands-on, Real objects   0 - ↑
```

Mastery Teaching Pyramid

throughout their day because of the number of different academic subjects being taught. Direct instruction often precedes a cooperative group or independent activity. Remembering that children learn through play, sensory activities, and first hand experiences is necessary for planning effective lessons. All learning should begin with a concrete or sensory activity.

So how would this work in a classroom? When we teach the standard that children should be able to identify rhyming words, many songs and nursery rhymes are sung, and the children name the rhyming words. Children listen to and sing the rhymes at the listening center, with and without pictures and books. A bucket appears on the table for the small group direct teaching lesson with the teacher. In the bucket are objects from the junk drawer at home that rhyme. The bucket might contain a ring and string, stuffed bear and a pear, lock and a sock, toy car and a jar, etc. Each item is identified and talked about and then grouped into rhyming pairs. The bucket is then placed in a learning center for children to play with independently.

After the concrete activity, the children should have semi-concrete or association activity with pictures, beginning to match the pictures of rhyming sounds. In the large or small direct instruction group, the children would read pictures and match the rhyming pairs, either through concentration or memory games. Children would also draw their own pictures to make rhyming picture books or cards.

The final step is for children to have the opportunity to work at the abstract or memory level with the standard. As children begin drawing their own pictures, they are asked to think of rhyming pairs and draw, write, or say the pairs from memory. Teachers may say one word, and the children give the rhyming word with no prompts or picture clues. For example, the teacher says, "What is a word that rhymes with door?" The child says "floor."

Integrated Units

Integrated units and themes give teachers a marvelous way to teach standards using problem solving skills with higher levels of thinking, differentiating the curriculum to meet the needs of individual students and providing constructivist/hands-on learning.

Topics are usually selected from science and social studies. All areas of the curriculum are addressed through the study. Standards in reading, language, math, physical education, the arts, social studies and science are taught and assessed. Children are involved in meaningful learning. Assessments and curriculum planning should include strategies and activities that meet the needs of all types of learners. Best practice strategies and programs can be used throughout the unit.

Teachers may plan units that include many standards and spend varying amounts of time with each unit. During the winter when the weather was always unsure, I planned one-day literature units using nursery rhymes and fairy tales in the event that instruction was interrupted. Standards taught were in letter/sound relationships, language comprehension through dramatization and rewriting endings, genres of literature, studies of cultures of other countries.

Other times a unit might last two weeks in order to give ample time for the children to explore and study all aspects of the topic. Teaching the habitats of animals and finding similarities in animals always led to a field trip to the zoo. Prior to the trip, several days were spent studying and researching animals that would be seen on the trip. Fiction and non-fiction books and stories were read, summarized, sequenced orally and with pictures and writing. Children demonstrated the movements of animals, drew pictures, painted, and designed murals. They counted by twos, added and categorized the animals by color, shape, size and scientific groups. Every curriculum area was used to learn about animals and teach standards.

Higher Order Thinking Skills (HOTS)

Bloom's Taxonomy of Higher Order Thinking orders the difficulty of the thinking process. Some refer to these steps as Productive Thinking. The base of Bloom's ladder is knowledge of a concept or subject. Sequentially, children must comprehend, compare similarities and differences, analyze, predict, synthesize, and finally make decisions. In the past, most of the learning and activity expected of children in school was at the knowledge and comprehension levels. The higher-level activities were reserved for "gifted and talented" children. Research shows that all children, given opportunities at the higher levels of the ladder, become better, more productive students and citizens. Creative children, not just the academically gifted children, often do very well with these types of problems.

Teachers must include daily opportunities for children to perform at higher levels. **Questioning Techniques** play a major role in the frequency of these opportunities. Teachers must take every opportunity to ask questions that are open-ended, that require more than a true/false or multiple-choice answer. Children should be describing, explaining, paraphrasing, summarizing, comparing, predicting, evaluating. Teachers can use opportunities in science, social studies, math, literature, and the arts to plan these activities and questions.

Parent Involvement

Parent involvement, being a partner in the teaching/learning process, is nothing new. Parents are the child's first teacher. Many schools have pre-school programs such as Parents As Teachers, HIPPY, Head Start and Pre-K, with specific parent components that make parent participation an integral part of the program.

When children leave pre-K, we need to maintain that parental enthusiasm and support. We need involved parents to have good students. Parents support their children by:

- Preparing them to enter school.
- Providing a time and place for reading, both to and with their child.
- Providing a time and place for completing homework.
- Talking and listening to the child.
- Taking their child to appropriate events and places in the community.
- Bringing their child to school on time.

Schools have a responsibility to the parent as well. Schools should provide many opportunities for parents to be welcome at school and give information about their child. These opportunities should happen throughout the school year and each school or center should be responsible for developing a parent involvement plan that is used by all teachers in the school or center.

Teaching Strategies

Some Ideas to Increase Parent Involvement & Participation

- Parent study groups on topics of interest or parenting issues.
- Interactive parent-child nights at school that provide parents with information, through hands-on methods and materials, about the curriculum and assessments being used with their children.
- *Doughnuts for Mom and Dad*, a class meeting with the teacher and parents explaining test scores and assessments at the end of the year. Parents are delighted to have the explanation about the tests and see the growth of their children.
- Opinion surveys that poll parents about the needs and outcomes of school programs.
- Parent surveys on the readiness of entering kindergarten children.
- PTO.
- Parent Advisory Groups.
- Parent/Teacher conferences at least twice a year, more often as needed.
- Parent representatives on School Improvement Planning Committees.
- Parent information systems with school web sights, monthly newsletters, signs.
- Teacher weekly reports and work folders.
- Open house.
- Informational newsletters on parenting and school topics.
- Volunteers in Schools, library, workroom, office, tutors, vision and hearing screenings, field day activities, room mothers, library inventory, Teacher Appreciation Day, Kindergarten Screening Aids, Red Ribbon Week activities, Field Trip chaperones.
- IDEA and 504 Conferences.
- Play Groups for pre-school children that include parent meetings.
- Public Meetings.
- Title 1 Meetings.

Notes

Chapter 6

Aligning Curriculum with Standards:
An Interdisciplinary/Integrated Thematic Unit for the Second Grade

We're finished with the theory. Now, let's see how an actual unit designed for the second grade would look. The following lesson plans were written under the direction of Dr. T. Roger Taylor as part of an interdisciplinary/integrated thematic unit by seven teachers (including me!) from the Ward Central Elementary School of the Cabot School District in Arkansas. I'm proud to tell you that they're teachers on my staff, and we're working together to provide the best education we can for the children of our school! We've used the benchmarks and standards for Arkansas, but you'll find the same type of standards and benchmarks in your state. We hope this unit will give you some ideas about how to take your state's standards and make them work for you and your children. It's an exciting journey into a new frontier in education. **Take a chance and give it a try!**

Many thanks to our unit authors:

Sheila Bray
Tonya Baldwin
Sharon White
Michele French

Makale Barnett
Kathy Buckmaster
Amy Vailes

A Second Grade Character Education Unit

Overarching Benchmarks/Goals for a Complete Unit of Study

Benchmark #1: Social Studies: People, Places, Environment—Students will demonstrate an understanding that people, cultures and systems are connected and that commonalities and diversities exist among them.

Benchmark #2: Social Science: Processes and Skills—Students will demonstrate critical thinking skills through research, reading, writing, speaking, listening and problem-solving.

Benchmark #3: Language Arts/Writing: The learner will be able to employ a wide range of strategies in writing and use different writing process elements appropriately to communicate with different audiences for a variety of purposes.

Benchmark #4: Language Arts/Reading: The learner will be able to comprehend, evaluate and respond to works of literature and other kinds of writing, which reflect his/her own culture and developing viewpoints as well as those of others.

SELF-RESPECT

State Standard #PPE. 1.5   Students will be able to analyze the effects of interactions between people and their environment.

Knowledge
Anticipatory Set: Read the following quote from Henry Wadsworth Longfellow: "The person who has self-respect is safe from others. That person wears a coat of armor that no one can cut through." Bring in several coats of armor. (Examples: turtle shell, hermit crab shell.)
Students Will: Discuss and define what it means to have self-respect (to appreciate and like yourself).

Comprehension
Students will defend or challenge in writing their feelings about the quote by Henry Wadsworth Longfellow.

Application
Anticipatory Set: Listen to the song "Respect" by Aretha Franklin and use a power point presentation on respect. (The presentation will demonstrate self-respect with works of art for body, mind and emotions.)
Students Will: Discuss ways to respect themselves.
Class/team product: Make a body map labeling ways to respect our bodies, mind and emotions.

Aligning Curriculum with Standards

Multicultural
Discuss the way that people show respect in different cultures.

Science Link
Plan a nutritious meal using the food pyramid to emphasize showing respect for your body.

School to Career
The P.E. teacher will talk with students about respecting one's body with exercise and model in P.E. class.

Higher Order Thinking Skills:
Anticipatory Set: Use flannel board as a visual aid when reading the book, *I Know an Old Lady Who Swallowed a Pie* by Alison Jackson.

Students Will: Analyze the behavior of the characters in the story for self-respect.

Class/team/Individual Product: Examine your daily schedule and list ways you show self-respect with body, mind and feelings. Illustrate one idea in each category.

Individual Journal Assignment
Think about your favorite hero. How does he or she show self-respect?

Homelink
Interview a family member. Ask three questions: How do they show self-respect to their body? How do they show self-respect to their mind? How do they show self-respect to their feelings?

TOLERANCE

State Standard #PPE. 1.6   Students will be able to distinguish similarities and differences among families and communities around the world.

Knowledge
Anticipatory Set: Read aloud the book, *Hooway for Wodney Wat*, by Helen Lester.

Students Will: State the meaning of tolerance and become aware of the relationship of tolerance to good character traits through a discussion of the book's characters.

Comprehension
Students will complete a character analysis of Wodney Wat using a graphic organizer.

Application
Anticipatory Set: Disabled guest speakers will visit the classrooms.

Students Will: Perform activities with a non-dominant side of the body. Examples: writing with the opposite hand, tying shoes with one hand, taking a trust walk blindfolded.

Class/team product: Discussion of feelings when using non-dominate body parts to complete a task.

Multicultural

Children will learn to sign their names using the sign language alphabet.

Science Link

Students will discuss the five senses and provide examples of how they are used by the body. What happens if one of these senses is absent?

School to Career

Occupational and physical therapists will visit each classroom to discuss disabilities.

Higher Order Thinking Skills

Anticipatory Set: Read *Penelope's Amazing Imperfect-People-Eating Machine* by fourth grade students at Village Elementary School.

Students Will: Construct an imperfect-people tolerator machine in teams.

Class/team/Individual Product: Students will describe and explain to the class how their machine will discover the strengths of imperfect people.

Individual Journal Assignment

Students will reflect and write about their individual strengths and weaknesses.

Homelink

Students will share their journal entries with their families.

HONESTY

State Standard #PPE. 1.7   Students will be able to use a variety of processes, such as thinking, listening, reading, writing and speaking to analyze interdependence.

Knowledge

Anticipatory Set: Show clip from *Liar Liar* (scene where Jim Carrey's character lies to his son).

Students Will: Tell the importance of being honest. Discuss how the son in *Liar Liar* felt when he was lied to by his father.

Comprehension

Divide class in half. One side of the class defends the father in *Liar Liar* and the other side will challenge the father. As the children debate, make a t-chart showing the pros and cons of parents being honest with their children.

Application

Anticipatory Set: Read aloud *The Big Fat Enormous Lie* by Marjorie Sharmat.

Aligning Curriculum with Standards

Students Will: Make a personal connection to *The Big Fat Enormous Lie*.

Class/team product: Students will write down a lie that they have told. They will design a lie monster and glue the lie on the monster. Students will be challenged to confront the person to whom the lie was told and give him/her the monster.

Multicultural

Read *The Boy Who Cried Wolf* (Dutch literature) to show children how honesty is an important characteristic of children in different countries.

Humanities Link

Discuss the term "false advertising." Give examples of times when students bought something and it was not what it was advertised to be.

School to Career

The music teacher will teach the song "Telling the Truth" by Loren K. Elms.

Higher Order Thinking Skills:

Anticipatory Set: Show clip from *Pinocchio* (scene where Pinocchio lies and his nose grows).

Students Will: Determine the dishonest behavior.

Class/team/Individual Product: Use the story *Miserable Millie* (from the series *Character Under Construction*) and building blocks to illustrate how one lie can lead to another and eventually tumble down.

Individual Journal Assignment

Describe a friend who is honest.

Homelink

Interview a family member about a time when they were tempted to tell a lie and tell what happened.

RESPONSIBILITY

State Standard #PPE. 1.1 *Students will be able to investigate how members of a family, school, community, state and nation depend on each other.*

Knowledge

Anticipatory Set: Sing "Rocking Responsibility" by Donna Forrest.

Students Will: Identify and name specific responsibilities at school and home on a list. Students will be able to define the term "responsibility."

Comprehension

Each student will convert his/her list of responsibilities into a book entitled "My Responsibilities."

Each page will feature one drawing and a short description of a responsibility.

Application

Anticipatory Set: Read the poem *A Teacher's Lament* by Kalli Dakos.

Students Will: Organize a display board portraying an adult family member's job or a job in the community.

Class/team product: Each display board will show responsibilities through photographs, drawings, and/or descriptive words.

Multicultural

Compare and contrast the responsibilities the students have now with the responsibilities that their grandparents had as children.

Humanities Link

Brainstorm and list responsibilities that community leaders have each day.

School to Career

Place display boards around the classroom or on a bulletin board entitled, "Jobs in Our Community." Students can research jobs on-line for posters.

Higher Order Thinking Skills

Anticipatory Set: Show clip from *Home Alone* (the scene where the main character realizes that he is home alone).

Students Will: Create a scenario where someone accepted or neglected their responsibility.

Class/team/Individual Product: In groups or pairs, students will produce the scenario and include the consequences that occurred because of their actions. They will role-play these scenarios for other students.

Individual Journal Assignment

Write about what would happen if you neglected or accepted one of your responsibilities. Reflect on the consequences or rewards.

Homelink

Make a responsibility chart and take it home to put on the refrigerator or in your room as a reminder.

COMPASSION

State Standard #W. 1.5   *Students will be able to write from experiences and thoughts.*

Knowledge

Anticipatory Set: Read aloud the book *Wilfrid Gordon McDonald Partridge* by Mem Fox.

Aligning Curriculum with Standards

Students Will: Develop an understanding of compassion. Make a list of ways students can show compassion to others through actions and words.

Comprehension

Share ways people have shown compassion in the past. Example: Teachers show compassion to their students by..., Mother Teresa...famous wealthy people, etc.

Application

Anticipatory Set: Show clip from *Fox and the Hound* (scene where Copper gets in front of owner's gun to protect the fox).

Students Will: Compile a list of feeling words.

Class/team product: Put each feeling word on a slip of paper and place all slips of paper in a can. Each student will pull a slip out and act out the feeling written on it. The rest of the class will try to guess the feeling displayed.

Multicultural

Students will show verbal and non-verbal expressions of compassion.

Humanities Link

Students will use literature, movies, songs, etc., to dramatize situations demonstrating compassion in groups or pairs.

School to Career

A veterinarian discusses the need for compassion in caring for animals. Download information on saving the whales.

Higher Order Thinking Skills

Anticipatory Set: Show clip from *Mary Poppins* (scene where old lady is feeding birds).

Students Will: Write and illustrate a card for an elderly person at a nursing home.

Class/team/Individual Product: Completed cards will be delivered to the nursing home.

Individual Journal Assignment

Students complete the following sentence frame: I have compassion when...

Homelink

Decide as a family to show kindness to someone in the community. Share the experience with the class.

COOPERATION

State Standard #R. 1.9   *Students will be able to establish purposes for reading, enjoyment, learning, modeling, sharing, performing, investigating and solving problems.*

Tt Uu Vv

Knowledge

Anticipatory Set: Show scene from *Parent Trap* (scene with the song "Let's Get Together").
Students Will: Recognize that many jobs can only be done by a group of people working together to achieve a common goal. They will learn why listening is important in group work. Students will work together to build a story by having each student contribute to the plot.

Comprehension

Students will make a t-chart of what to do and what not to do when cooperating with others on building a story as a class. Examples: Do listen to other children while they are talking, Don't interrupt others when they are talking.

Application

Anticipatory Set: Read aloud *The Little Red Hen*.
Students Will: Construct a story map.
Class/team product: Complete a story map on the plot of *The Little Red Hen*.

Multicultural

Compare and contrast breads from three different countries. Research how the three countries cooperate in economics, farming, and government. Draw a web. (Suggested countries: Mexico, Germany, Japan)

Mathematics Link

Measure the ingredients for making a loaf of bread.

School to Career

Take pictures with a digital camera of the steps in making bread. Sequence the pictures to show how to make bread.

Higher Order Thinking Skills

Anticipatory Set: Show clip from *Remember the Titans* (scene where the players are working together at the football camp).
Students Will: Work together to bake bread.
Class/team/Individual Product: Students will divide their group into different jobs and complete the bread recipe.

Individual Journal Assignment

Respond to the statement, "I work and play well with others."

Homelink

Students will play the card game, "Compare" or "Double Compare" (from *Math Investigations*) with a family member. This game enriches number sense in cooperative play.

Aligning Curriculum with Standards

INTEGRITY

State Standard #SSPS 1.2   Students will be able to recognize and discuss different perspectives in current and past issues.

Knowledge
Anticipatory Set: Show clip from *Stand by Me* (scene where Chris tells story about being dishonest around the campfire).
Students Will: Conduct a class discussion on what a person of integrity is and stands for.

Comprehension
Divide the class into small groups. Have each group develop a list of do's and don'ts for being a person of integrity.

Application
Anticipatory Set: Read aloud *Dr. Desoto*.
Students Will: Discuss doing the right thing, even when you are scared.
Class/team product: Students will produce a list of personal principles, or basic beliefs, that they would not compromise, no matter what. Students will select one of these principles and write a story (real or imagined), describing a time they did something courageous by standing up for this principle.

Multicultural
Read aloud *Lon Po Po* (Chinese tale) by Ed Young.

Humanities Link
Conduct a discussion on *Lon Po Po*. Lon Po Po jeopardizes her integrity, so she ends up with the wolf.

School to Career
Have a high school athlete, band member, cheerleader or student body leader discuss choices he/she makes to maintain his/her integrity as a role mode/community leader.

Higher Order Thinking Skills
Anticipatory Set: Show clip from *Harriet the Spy* (scene where Harriet loses all of her friends because she has been spying on them).
Students Will: Determine the characteristics of integrity that they would want to have.
Class/team/Individual Product: Compose and sign a contract with yourself on how you will not compromise your integrity.

Individual Journal Assignment
Respond to this question: "Is being thought of as someone with integrity important to you? Why or why not?"

Tt Uu-Vv

Homelink

Have an adult help the student find newspaper articles about people who the student thinks have integrity and people who the student thinks do not. Bring these articles to share with the class.

FRIENDSHIP

State Standard #W 1.5.B1   *Students will be able to write brief personal narratives that are logically sequenced and describe people, objects and events in school.*

Knowledge

Anticipatory Set: Listen to the song "You've Got a Friend" from the movie *Toy Story*.

Students Will: Describe the importance of positive friendship and learn how to be a good friend. They will develop open-ended questions to find out about a classmate.

Comprehension

Students will interview a classmate to find out about that child and compile the interviews into a class book.

Application

Anticipatory Set: Read aloud *Best Friends* by Steven Kellog and listen to the song "That's What Friends Are For" by Dionnne Warwick.

Students Will: Discuss the qualities of good friendships and characteristics.

Class/team product: Students will write an acrostic poem with their names, outlining friendship qualities or characteristics.

Multicultural

Learn the words for friendship in several languages.

Mathematics Link

Play the game "Sums to 10" (from *Math Investigations*) in pairs.

School to Career

Use a digital camera to take pictures of interviewer and interviewee (from the comprehension exercise) to add to the class book of friends.

Higher Order Thinking Skills

Anticipatory Set: Read aloud *Ira Sleeps Over*.

Students Will: Write a recipe for friendship using a recipe card.

Class/team/Individual Product: Write a recipe for keeping friendships with people who no longer live close to you.

Individual Journal Assignment

Reflect upon what characteristics you have that would make you a good friend.

Homelink

Share the acrostic poem on friendship with a family member.

TEN ETHICAL DILEMMAS FOR A CHARACTER EDUCATION UNIT

State Standard #R.2.1.   *Students will demonstrate a willingness to use reading to continue to learn, to communicate and to solve problems independently.*

These dilemmas offer possible scenarios for role-play, discussion and the writing center.

1. There are several students talking and the teacher says, "I need the students who are talking without permission to go move their card." You know that you were talking without permission. What do you do?

2. You see your best friend's older brother smoking at the back of the bus. What do you do?

3. There is a child in your class that is on a behavior plan. He received three warnings before he was told to move his card. What do you do when you only received one warning and were told to move your card?

4. You were chosen to be the student ambassador for your class. You are very shy and feel uncomfortable about being an ambassador. What do you do?

5. You are writing new lyrics for a song about a step in the Stop and Think Program at school. You are very excited and have written two steps for the Stop and Think Program. Your best friend didn't write his and he wants to use your extra step. What do you do?

6. It is time to go to recess. Most of the class has left the room. You notice that one of your classmates has had a bathroom accident. What do you do?

7. You are chosen to be the counter for the students using the swings. You counted to twenty but one student on the swing says that you are only on twelve. What do you do?

8. You have been assigned to work with a student with multiple disabilities. Your friends have begun to tease you about your partner. What do you do?

9. In your cooperative group, there is one student who has not contributed anything to the assignment. It is now time to turn in your group assignment. What do you do?

10. There is an obese classmate assigned to your team for Track and Field Day. You are a very competitive player. You have won first place in every event for the last two years. What would you do?

CHARACTER EDUCATION

INDEPENDENT RESEARCH PROJECTS (I-SEARCH PROJECTS)

The following 18 projects may be used for cooperative group activities or may be written for use on task cards in learning centers for groups or individuals. They were developed for all students; however, many students need to be involved in enrichment activities that provide further experiences in literacy.

1. People believe that if you are nice to others, they will always be nice to you. Each group or individual will create a skit demonstrating real life situations where this belief may not be a reality. (*Drama Center*)

2. Children will create two to four puppets and create a script for the puppets that focuses on one of the following character traits: honesty, integrity respect, cooperation, citizenship or friendship. (*Art Center*)

3. Children will write a fairy tale, choosing a story line with good characters conforming to bad or bad characters conforming to good. Example: *The Girl Who Washed in Moonlight* (*Writing Center*)

4. Using blocks, children will create a maze that has roadblocks. At each roadblock, children will write situations that happen in their lives at school and at home where they must make decisions about what to do. As children use the maze as a game, the roadblocks are opened if they make good choices and they continue through the maze. If a bad choice is made, the child will have to choose a different direction in order to get to the end of the maze. The good choices may be written down and used for discussion at a later time. (*Building Center*)

5. Children gather data through observation, surveys and interviews in order to write a new rule for their school. Data is shared with graphs and summaries. Introduce the new rule during the next six week's assembly. (*Writing Center*)

6. Use Picasso prints to research art impressionism. Children will design and title their own artwork depicting good character traits that will be displayed in the school art gallery. (*Art Center*)

7. Children will design their own bumper stickers with positive action statements. Example: It takes less muscle to SMILE than frown. (*Art Center*)

8. Using one of the literature pieces of this unit, children will create a photo essay. Instruction on how to use digital cameras should be given if needed. (*Art Center*)

9. Children will conduct an historical search on how people in the past settled disagreements. They will predict how disagreements will be settled in the future and place these predictions on a timeline. (*Reading Center*)

10. Using a scenario in which a popular person discusses the mistake he/she made and how the mistake affected his/her reputation, children will develop an interview segment and act it out. Example: Sammy Sosa talking about the use of a cork bat in a major league baseball game. (*Drama Center*)

11. Children compose a song that expresses feelings when making a difficult choice. (*Music Center*)

12. Children develop a training manual for incorporating good character in everyday life. They should use numerous situations and examples. (*Writing Center*)

13. Children produce a television program or documentary on creative people. They should include many examples of problem solving and inventions. (*Drama Center*)

14. Children will review movies that demonstrate examples of chaos in school, then write an editorial for the newspaper justifying the need for order in the classroom. (*Writing Center*)

15. Children use the library and web to develop a bibliography of articles, books, stories, etc. on "getting along." (*Reading Center*)

16. Children create a listening center in the classroom where other students can spend time listening to stories dealing with character issues. (*Listening Center*)

17. Children study several travel brochures and develop a brochure to invite travelers to visit the fantasy "Character Island." They should include picture, attractions and activities. (*Writing Center*)

18. Children take pictures to develop a slide show, create a sculpture or produce a power point presentation to depict their feelings while cooperating with classmates on project. (*Technology Center*)

Other Learning Center Activities:

Listening Center
Tapes of books, stories and songs

Word Center
Develop a word wall of character and related words

Science Center
Include study and activities of the five senses, food pyramid and exercises for healthy bodies

Art Center
Incorporate materials to make friendship and mood bracelets

Cooking Center
Have bread recipes and ingredients to measure and make bread

CHARACTER EDUCATION VOCABULARY
Cultural/Literacy/Spelling List

Accepted
Acrostic
Alice in Wonderland (title)
Ambassador
Analyze
Appropriate
Attributes
Bar graph
Blindfold
Brainstorming
Characteristics
Cheerleader
Citizenship
Class president
Coat of armor
Community
Compare
Compassion
Compose
Compromise
Consequences
Contract
Contrast
Cookie Crisp cereal
Cooperation
Culture
Dennis the Menace
Digital camera
Disability
Dramatize
Election
Empathy
Environment
Feeling
Friendship

Generalize
Geometry
Getting along
Height
Henry Wadsworth Longfellow
Hero
Hexagon
Home Alone (title)
Honesty
Inappropriate
Informative
Integrity
Interviewee
Interviewer
Investigate
Job
Journal
Length
Lie
Local government
Manners
Mayor measurement
Meter stick
Metric system
Neglected
Non-standard
Obese
Octagon
Pamphlet
Pentagon
Perimeter
Personality
Phrases
Pinocchio
Playground

Police Chief
Principle
Procedures
Qualities
Recognize
Rectangle
Registered voter
Responsibility
Role model
Role-play
Rulers
Rules
S.L.I.P. (solve, label, illustrate, paragraph)
Scenario
School counselor
Self-respect
Simba
Situations
Sphere
Square
Standard
STOP and THINK
Student ambassador
Summarize
Survey
The Buttercream Gang (title)
The Recess Queen (title)
Transportation
Triangle
Venn diagram
Veterinarian
Width
Willy Wonka

Aligning Curriculum with Standards

CHARACTER EDUCATION UNIT RESOURCES

Bibliography-Teacher/Professional Books and Resources

Brooks, David. *Lessons in Character*. Young People's Press, 1996.

Burns, Marilyn. *Math and Literature (K-3)*. Math Solutions Publications, 1992.

Forrest, Donna. *Character Under Construction*. Youth Light Inc., 2000.

Getting Better at Getting Along, Grades 2-4. Sunburst Communications, 1992.

Getting Better at Getting Along Role-Play Cards. Sunburst Communications, 1992.

Greer, Colin and Kohl, Herbert. *A Call to Character*. Harper Perennial, 1995.

Holub. *My First Book of Sign Language*. Troll, 1998.

I Will Be Your Friend: Songs and Activities for Young Peacemakers. Teaching Tolerance, 2003.

Investigations, Grade 2. Dale Seymour Publications, 2002.

Knoblock, Kathleen. *Character Education, Grades 2-4*. Instructional Fair, 1997.

Knoff, Howard. *Implementing Social Skills: Training in the Classroom*. Institute for School Reform, Integrated Services and Child Mental Health, 1997.

Lansky, Bruce and Carpenter, Stephen. *Kids Pick the Funniest Poems*. Meadowbrook, 1991.

Mannix, Darlene. *Social Skills Activities for Special Children*. Prentice Hall, 1993.

McGinnis, Ellen and Goldstein, Arnold. *Skillstreaming in Early Childhood*. Research Press, 1990.

McGinnis, Ellen and Goldstein, Arnold. *Skillstreaming the Elementary School Child*. Research Press, 1984.

Newbury, Ken. *Character Word of the Week*. Young People's Press, 1998.

Popov, Linda. *The Virtues Project Educator's Guide*. Jalmar Press, Inc., 2000.

Romano, Lee and Parker, Amy. *Captain Music-Character Counts...So Do I!* Captain Music, Inc., 2000.

Schilling, Dianne. *Fifty Activities for Teaching Emotional Intelligence*. Innerchoice Publishing, 1996.

Sheffield, Stephanie. *Math and Literature*. Math Solutions Publications, 1995.

Wise Quotes: Skills for Building Positive Character. Legacy Learning, 1995.

Wise Quotes: Simple Sayings That Teach Good Choices. Legacy Learning, 1995.

Bibliography-Student Books (for classroom use)

Bridwell, Norman. *Clifford's Manners*. Scholastic, Inc., 1987.

Browne, Philippa-Alys. *African Animals ABC's*. Sierra Club Books, 1995.

Carlson, Nancy. *How to Lose All Your Friends*. Puffin Books, 1997.

Cazet, Denys. *Never Spit on Your Shoes*. Orchard Books, 1990.

Couric, Katie. *The Brand New Kid*. Doubleday, 2000.

Fourth Grade Students at Village Elementary School. *Penelope's Amazing Imperfect-People-Eating Machine*. Willow Press, 1998.

Hutchins, Pat. *The Doorbell Rang*. Pearson Learning, 1989.

Jackson, Alison. *I Know an Old Lady Who Swallowed a Pie.* Penguin Books, 2002.

Kellog, Steven. *Best Friends.* Dial, 1986

Lobel, Arnold. *Frog and Toad Are Friends.* Harper and Row Publishers, 1970.

Mayer, Gina and Mercer. *Just Say Please.* A Golden Book, 1998.

McQueen, Lucinda. *The Little Red Hen.* Scholastic, 1987.

Munsinger, Lynn. *Hooway for Wodney Wat.* Houghton Mifflin Co, 1999.

O'Neill, Alexis and Huliska-Beith, Laura. *The Recess Queen.* Scholastic, Inc., 2002.

Pike, Debi and Raffi. *Like Me and You.* Crown Publishers, 1994

Sharmal, Marjorie. *The Big Fat Enormous Lie.* Library Binding, 1999.

Steig, William. *Doctor DeSoto.* Farrar Strans and Giroux, 1982

Waber, Bernard. *Ira Sleeps Over.* Houghton Mifflin Co., 1973.

Young, Ed. *Lon Po Po*, Philomel Books, 1989.

Educational Films/Videos

Just Like Dad. Sandstar Family Entertainment.

Kids for Character. Character Counts.

The Buttercream Gang. Feature Films for Families, 1991.

We Can Work Together. Sunburst Communications.

Commercial Films/Videos

Caution: Before using films and videos, check with your Media Coordinator to ensure that all appropriate licenses and approval for classroom use are completed.

Alice in Wonderland	*Parent Trap*
An Officer and a Gentleman	*Pinocchio*
Forrest Gump	*Remember the Titans*
Harriet the Spy	*Rigoletto*
Home Alone	*Stand by Me*
Liar, Liar	*Toy Story*
Lion King	*Willie Wonka and the Chocolate Factory*
Madeline Manners	*Wizard of Oz*
Mary Poppins	*The Wrong Way Kid: I'm not Oscar's Friend*
Matilda	*Anymore.*

Literature/Language Arts (placed on reserve for students to check out)

Bang, Molly. *When Sophie Gets Angry, Really, Really Angry.....* Scholastic, Inc., 1999.

Berenstain, Stan and Jan. *The Berenstain Bears and the Trouble with Friends.* Random House, 1986.

Berenstain, Stan and Jan. *The Berenstain Bears Get in a Fight.* Random House, 1982.

Berenstain, Stan and Jan. *The Berenstain Bears Go Out for the Team.* Random House, 1986.

Chapman, Susan. *The Get Along Gang and the Cry Baby.* Scholastic, Inc., 1984.

Aligning Curriculum with Standards

Cosby, Bill. *The Best Way to Play*. Scholastic, Inc., 1997.
Cosby, Bill. *The Meanest Things to Say*. Scholastic, Inc., 1997.
Gaines, Isabel. *Pooh's Best Friend*. Disney Press, 1998.
Hoban, Lillian. *Like Me and You*. Crown Publishers, Inc., 1985.
Lucado, Max. *Just the Way You Are*. Scholastic, Inc., 1992.
Munteam, Michaela. *I Have a Friend*. Golden Press, 1981.
Parton, Dolly. *Coat of Many Colors*. Scholastic, Inc., 1992.
Payne, Lauren. *We Can Get Along*. Free Spirit, 1987.
Ross, Dave. *A Book of Friends*. Scholastic, Inc., 1999.
Shannon, David. *David Gets in Trouble*. Blue Sky Press, 2002.
Shannon, David. *David Goes to School*. Blue Sky Press, 1999.
Sharmat, Marjorie. *I'm Terrific*. Scholastic Book Services, 1977.
Stevenson, Jocelyn. *Best Friends*. Muppet Press, 1984.

Poetry

Could Have Been Worse, Bill Dodds
If I Were the Ruler of the World, Bill Dodds
Rules to Live By, Linda Knaus
Sarah Cynthia Sylvia Stout Would Not Take the Garbage Out, Shel Silverstein
Suzanna Socked Me, Jack Prelutsky
Teacher's Lament, Kalli Dakos
The Leader, Roger McGough

Music

"A Song for the Children", Becky and Harry Manfredin
"Friendship", Cole Porter
"I Just Can't Wait to Be King", from the Lion King
"Like Me and You", Raffi and Debi Pike
"Respect", Aretha Franklin
"Rockin Responsibility", Donna Forrest
"Signs", Tesla
"Stop, In the Name of Love", Diana Ross and the Supremes
"Telling the Truth", Loren Elms
"That's What Friends are For", Dionne Warwick
"Think", Aretha Franklin
"Ward Central Pride Song", Tonya Baldwin (Substitute your school's song here!)
"Wheels on the Bus"
"You've Got a Friend", Carole King

Notes

References and Resources

Arkansas Division of Child Care and Early Childhood Education. (1996). *Arkansas early childhood education framework: Benchmarks with strategies/activities for three and four year old children.* Little Rock, AR: Arkansas Department of Human Services

Bredekamp, S. and Copple, C. (1997). *Developmentally appropriate practice in early childhood programs.* Washington, DC: National Association for the Education of Young Children.

Bredekamp, S. and Rosegrant (1992). *Reaching potentials: Appropriate curriculum and assessment for young children* (Vol. 1). Washington, DC: National Association for the Education of Young Children.

Bronson, M. (1995). *The right stuff for children birth to eight.* Washington, DC: National Association for the Education of Young Children.

Brown, D. and Wright, B. (2002) *Picture this: A framework for quality care and education for children from three to five.* Little Rock, AR: Arkansas Department of Human Services, Division of Child Care and Early Childhood Education.

Campbell, R. (Ed.) (1998). *Facilitating pre-school literacy.* Newark, DE: International Reading Association.

Carbo, M. (1997). *What every principal should know about teaching reading.* Syosset, NY: National Reading Styles Institute.

Covey, S. (1992). *Principle-centered leadership.* New York: Simon & Schuster.

Covey, S. (1990). *The seven habits of highly effective people.* New York: Simon & Schuster.

Diller, D. (2003) *Literacy work stations: Making centers work.* Portland, ME: Stenhouse Publishers.

Dodge, D.T. and Colker, L (1998). *The creative curriculum for early childhood.* (3rd ed.). Washington, DC: Teaching Strategies.

Dorn, L., French, C., and Jones, T. (1998) *Apprenticeship in literacy transitions across reading and writing.* Portland, ME: Stenhouse Publishers.

Dufour, R. and Eaker, R. (1992). *Professional learning communities at work: Best practices for enhancing student achievement.* Bloomington, IN: National Education Service.

Dufour, R. and Eaker, R. (1998). *Creating the new American school.* Bloomington, IN: National Education Service.

Early Childhood-Head Start Task Force. (2002). *Teaching our youngest: A guide for preschool teachers and child care and family providers.* US Department of Education and US Department of Health and Human Services. Washington, DC.

Educational Testing Service. (1995). *Arkansas model for pathwise classroom mentoring/observation.* Princeton, NJ.

Elkind, D. (1987). *Miseducation: Preschoolers at risk.* New York: Knopf.

Grant, J. (1998). *Developmental education in an era of high standards.* Rosemont, NJ: Modern Learning Press.

Healey, J. (1987). *Your child's growing mind.* New York: Doubleday.

Johnson, S. (1998). *Who moved my cheese?* New York: Putnam Pub Group

Leonard, A. (1997). *I spy something! A practical guide to classroom observations of young children.* Little Rock, AR: Southern Early Childhood Association.

Levine, M. (2002). *A mind at a time.* New York: Simon & Schuster

Lezotte, L. W. (1992). *Creating the total quality effective school.* Okemos, MI: Effective Schools Products.

Lunden, J. (1997). *Healthy living.* New York: Crown Publishers.

Lunden, J. (2001). *Wake-up calls.* New York: McGraw-Hill.

Lundin, S., Paul, H., and Christenson, J. (2000). *Fish: A remarkable way to boost morale, performance and results.* New York: Hyperion Press.

MacDonald, S. (1997). *The portfolio and its use: A road map for assessment.* Little Rock, AR: Southern Early Childhood Association.

Marzano, R. (2002). *What works in schools: Translating research into action.* Alexandria, VA: AS Curriculum Development.

Maslow, A.H. (1970). *Motivation and personality.* (2nd ed.). New York: Harper & Row.

Parkes, B. (2000). *Read it again.* Portland, ME: Stenhouse Publishers.

Reeves, D. (2002). *The leader's guide to standards: A blueprint for educational equity and excellence.* San Francisco: Jossey-Bass.

Reeves, D. (1998). *Standards, assessment and accountability.* Phoenix: NCSI.

Shaw, J. (1990). *Growing and learning: Ideas for teachers of young children.* Little Rock, AR: Southern Early Childhood Association.

Stevenson, M. F. and Zigler, E. (1999) *Schools of the 21st century: Linking child care and education.* Boulder, CO: Westview Press.

Swick, K. (1991). *Teacher-parent partnerships to enhance school success in early childhood programs.* Washington, DC: National Education Association.

Underwood, K. (2002). *Put reading in arkansas first.* Little Rock, AR: Arkansas Department of Education.

Wirtz, P. and Schumacher, B. (2003). *Menu for successful parent and family involvement.* Little Rock, AR: Southern Early Childhood Association.

Zemelman, S., Daniels, H., and Hyde, A. (1998) *Best practice: New standards for teaching and learning in america's schools.* (2nd ed.). Portsmouth, NH: Heineman.